GOD'S ISLAND

Gregory Motton
GOD'S ISLAND

OBERON BOOKS
LONDON

First published in French as *L'Isle de Dieu* in 2000 by Théatrâles.

First published in English in 2001 by Oberon Books Ltd.
(incorporating Absolute Classics)
521 Caledonian Road, London N7 9RH
Tel: 020 7607 3637 / Fax: 020 7607 3629

e-mail: oberon.books@btinternet.com

A catalogue record for this book is available from the British Library.

ISBN: 9781840021905

Cover design: Andrzej Klimowski

Typography: Richard Doust

Characters

GOD
LUCIFER
MARY
ESAU
JACOB
REBECCA
ISAAC
ANGEL
BROTHER
to Rachel
RACHEL
LABAN
LEAH
GABRIEL
JOSEPH
NURSE Goodwoman
DONKEY
MRS SPAM
A SPY
A MOCKER
MR WHEELWRIGHT
the inventor of the wheel
JESUS
COMMUNICATOR
LADY COUNCILLOR
MAN
JUDAS
HEROD
PILATE

ACT ONE

Scene 1

GOD: Well, Lucifer? How have you dealt with Noah?

LUCIFER: I sent the storm upon their necks, chased him and his chickens up the gang plank, wetted his bald pate and crammed the cattle, man and beast into their boat

GOD: And the rest?

LUCIFER: I drowned them, as you said. Some were swimming along with sofas and chairs floating in the muck but…they didn't last very long

GOD: Well done my fairy

LUCIFER: Why, O Great God, do you do such terrible magic upon the earth so as to drown it and kill all living things and creeping things so that nothing is left save poor Noah and his boat and his sons and their wives and their cattle and menagerie of creeping things and beasts.

GOD: So great is My rage Lucifer, for their wickedness, for they have displaced Me and speak My name no more and I am forgotten amongst men, so that in ten generations there has only been one good man, Enoch, whom I would not let die but took him to Me for he walked with Me. The rest I have let die and they have passed out their time upon the earth whence they have banished My name until now that I have gone down amongst them with My floods and storms and waters to destroy them, then they remember Me by My magic which they fear

LUCIFER: But having destroyed the earth once, why do You bring them back to it for they are no better than before, but are bigger fools and drunkards than ever, so that Noah is a clown naked in his tent before his sons,

Abraham makes himself rich by pimping his wife before the heathen and a bigger fool there never has been.

GOD: You will see how I run them this way and that; for that same iniquity and falseness they showed to Me they will use upon each other a thousand fold, so that the earth to them is a blind isle of fiends and tricks and its elements a host of savage fanged beasts unto them, and yea, their own lives will be like unto black dungeons filled with horrors, or shall be empty plains they must cross neither knowing an east nor a west, nor sun nor moon, illumined only from moment to moment with the bright sudden flashes of their own terror or greed, for they will know no peace nor no god neither, for when they look for me they will find only themselves, for I will make myself as like unto them as the stone is like unto their hearts – When they say 'Lord Lord, is it your face there in the darkness we see?' I shall say 'Yes!, run this way and that way' and they will run from one shadow to the next, and when they turn to me they shall be like a dog barking at the mirror. This is the prophesy of the Lord!

LUCIFER: Praise be to God!

GOD: Amen

LUCIFER: How will it end? Will they never again be soothed by your true spirit? Will they always be monkeys?

GOD: No end can there be until you and I are also monkeys, and are known by different names, denied and then forgotten. This is the prophesy of the Lord!

And so it goes on.

Scene 2

MARY: Eloachim, Father, why is what I do important to me but not to you? When I was a child with my toys you smiled down upon me, but I fought with those building bricks. Now I am a woman, you still smile down upon me and I fight with my life. And I say 'Hello Pappa, its me' and I say my name to remind you. And you say to yourself; 'Hmm, this is one of my children because she calls me Pappa (father) but which one of them can it be? Ah, it is you Frederick, or James or poor St John. Is it you St Thomas the lawyer, or little Theresa?' But father I am myself and I say to you Father It is I. And you pause in silence for you know not who it is you are speaking with.

GOD: You are afraid, Mary my child, and lonely

MARY: I am lonely because you never loved me

GOD: How can you know I never loved you? This you can never really know. That, I would say, is one of the features of being alive

MARY: Then I wish to be dead

GOD: But my beautiful daughter, you will throw away the gift of yourself I have given to you

MARY: Yes I may throw it away because I am worthless in your eyes. I'll see how it goes. I am indifferent to life. I may throw it down this well. Or I may not. I could be a lawyer. Or my books could fall down upon my head and kill me – all the better.

GOD: Can you imagine how lonely it is to love you as I do? And do nothing for you. To tell no-one. To always hide it. To give you nothing. To make you unhappy.

MARY: What would you do for me?

GOD: I'd like to come down from heaven and make you my wife. Then we'd live together with beautiful children with fish faces who looked like you, in an old villa in the flat country to the east and you'd earn the money and I'd paint pictures at home on the walls like you used to when you were little, remember?

MARY: Yes. That was my poor mother's house, you were never there. In your house I could never touch anything

GOD: I imagine we would have great dinner parties and in the evenings we'd lead our guests out along the roads to see the frogs in the ditches. You'd sing your funny songs to them and try to make me dance, and I'd laugh at you and smoke and drink red wine.

MARY: You are cruel. I never asked you to tell me this

GOD: Can't we dream together?

MARY: No because I only have one life

GOD: I have many but I can live none of them myself. It's even worse for me than it is for you.

MARY: You have destroyed me with this love of yours. From this day I shall call you Don Juan as all my friends do. 'Has Don Juan dropped in recently from the skies on his bicylette, in his man-powered flying machine?' they ask. Ha ha ha.

GOD: Don't you remember my love letters?

MARY: Love letters? Oh those! Those threats and cajolements? Those criticisms? Those. – Your negativity is the closest you ever get to poetry. It was so – out of proportion. Didn't anyone tell you how simple love could be?

GOD: No. I have suffered much on that account

MARY: And I have suffered on account of you telling me I would be better off in a desert or jumping down a well

GOD: Whatever possessed me to say that?

MARY: You put these ideas into my head and they stay there.

Scene 3

GOD: Lucifer, whatever are you doing?

LUCIFER: (*Quietly.*) I'm drilling a hole

GOD: Why? Why are you doing that?

LUCIFER: To make Death leak out

GOD: Leak? Leak where?

LUCIFER: I don't know. Into You?

GOD: What? You are trying to kill Me?

LUCIFER: Yes.

GOD: You are trying to kill God?

LUCIFER: Yes.

GOD: But I am dead already. Am I not Lord of Death's kingdom? Where do you get your ideas from?

LUCIFER: From somewhere inside of me. Sometimes I don't know what I'm doing, It is as if I am in a dream. Why am I drilling a hole in You, I don't know?

GOD: Maybe you wanted to steal Death from Me?

LUCIFER: Yes, that's it

GOD: Is it because you would like to die, Lucifer?

LUCIFER: Am I alive then that I can die?

GOD: I made you so you are alive, but, as for dying, I never thought of it

LUCIFER: If I die then will I be like You?

GOD: No, I will never die, can never die.

LUCIFER: But You are dead.

GOD: Yes, but I have never died. I was never alive. Always dead. Death is where I live.

LUCIFER: Aren't You afraid being so alone and never able to die?

GOD: But I have you to keep Me company

LUCIFER: No please, not forever! Promise me You'll let me die one day

GOD: Why have you never asked Me about this before?

LUCIFER: I was afraid what the answer might be. It's one thing to be God and never die, but to be only me, only Lucifer... I don't have sufficient love for myself to be alone with myself forever

GOD: Poor Lucifer

LUCIFER: Admit it, I'm the unluckiest creature ever created.

GOD: You are the only creature ever created

LUCIFER: Exactly

GOD: Forgive Me Lucifer

LUCIFER: I feel the need to Blaspheme

GOD: You already have

End of Act One.

ACT TWO

Scene 1

ESAU: May I sit down beside you Jacob, next to you and
your fire?

JACOB: Yes Esau, you may

ESAU: I shall take off my boots and warm my feet

JACOB: Do you have water?

ESAU: Sand

JACOB: Hungry?

ESAU: Starving

JACOB: I have made this lovely soup

Long pause.

Would you like some?

ESAU: Yes, I'm exhausted from hunting all day. I need
something to revitalise me

JACOB: Do you feel drained?

ESAU: Yes, drained

JACOB: I'd like you to sell me your birthright Esau.

ESAU: Would you? What exactly do you mean by that?

JACOB: Well, you were the first-born, by a few moments,
but nevertheless. You must have either pushed me out of
the way in the womb or, by pure chance you were just
the first to come out. As a result you stand to inherit
more than me, and to have authority over me when our
father Isaac dies.

ESAU: I see. Don't you like that, Jacob?

JACOB: No, I don't mind that. None of it really matters in practise at all. It's the idea of it that always bothers me. It seems unfair.

ESAU: Yes, I suppose it is.

JACOB: To be honest, I would like to be the one who had been born first.

ESAU: That's the one part you can't actually change

JACOB: What's that?

ESAU: I said –

JACOB: Look Esau, why don't you just sell me your birthright. You'd still inherit almost as much as me, and, well its only prestige you'd be losing, and a little authority. It hardly matters.

ESAU: I don't know Jacob. I know it hardly matters, but I don't know

JACOB: Why? Why don't you know? Do you think there's something else we haven't mentioned?

ESAU: No

JACOB: Well if you do, come on, out with it! Speak up, I'd love to hear it. Because I can't imagine what else there could be

ESAU: No, I don't think there is anything

JACOB: Nothing at all?

ESAU: No, I don't think so

JACOB: No secret reason why you feel you'd like to keep this advantage over me. No hidden benefits.

ESAU: No, its just that –

JACOB: What?

ESAU: It would feel wrong to give it away

JACOB: Wrong? Why? You haven't earned it have you?

ESAU: No

JACOB: There's no particular merit in you that makes you more deserving of it than me?

ESAU: Not that I can see.

JACOB: Well then!

ESAU: But that's just why I feel that to give it away might be wrong. Because perhaps, perhaps it was *meant* to be so.

JACOB: *Meant* to be so? By whom?

ESAU: By... God.

JACOB: You think God may have picked you out for some special destiny which hitherto there is no sign of?

ESAU: It's possible

JACOB: You think that? What a surprise! I had no idea you were like this. And for this reason you could not consider selling your birthright to your brother who really wants it?

ESAU: I didn't say I wouldn't consider it

JACOB: Oh, you want me to beg? I can tell you Esau, if I was the one who by nothing other than pure chance had landed up with this birthright I wouldn't have used it in the way you do to lord it over me. You want me to go on my bended knees? Would that satisfy you?

ESAU: No, you don't have to do that. It means nothing, Neither one of us deserves it any more than the other

JACOB: That's fine for you to say. But you'll keep it just the same is that it?

ESAU: Well, no, no I needn't. I could give it to you I suppose.

JACOB: Give it? I didn't say give it. If you really believe you have no more right to it than me, it's not yours to give.

ESAU: Alright, what else then?

JACOB: Sell it. Chance has decreed you have the birthright. Chance has also decreed that I have this pot of soup and that you should be hungry. So you sell me the birthright for this bowl of soup.

ESAU: I thought you were going to give me the soup anyway?

JACOB: Well, you just offered me the birthright

ESAU: Did I? You offered me the soup because I was hungry

JACOB: You think your hunger gives you the right to the soup?

ESAU: If you like

JACOB: You could be right. I'd like to think about that. Another time though, not now. Because now we're talking about this birthright. I mean, perhaps my hunger for it gives me the right to it, have you considered that?

ESAU: Yes, it did occur to me

JACOB: Oh it did? Well then? Might it not be that this special destiny you suspect lies hidden within it in some way may actually belong, not to the great lump who shoved his way out of the womb first, and who hardly thinks about it, who hardly considers the advantages given to him, but belongs to the one who spends his whole days in anguish over it and who wakes up in a sweat sometimes because he feels his life has been ruined by a fluke, the one who has a *real* vision of a destiny that might just be his if it weren't for this one hindrance, this one anomaly that could be rectified

ESAU: I think you probably know that the largest part of me doesn't even want it. Not just that but anything. Family, wealth, mother, father, brother. I'd rather be alone. I'd rather be free. I don't want to think about any of it. I want to be on my own hunting in the forest. None of it means anything to me at all. You probably knew this about me?

JACOB: Yes, I do. Or I've always suspected it. Of course, it hurts me. And I feel a sense of outrage on behalf of our parents because of it. You feel no gratitude or loyalty to them do you?

ESAU: No, they are like strangers to me.

JACOB: Then for God's sake let me have what is rightfully mine and relieve yourself of the burden of the responsibility you are not equal to and don't want. Don't think I can't see the hunger in you Esau. You are a man of the plain, a man of adventure, born perhaps to be an exile. In a foreign land is perhaps where you will find yourself and your own kind. It is as if you are a misfit here, but that elsewhere you will fit in perfectly.

ESAU: You'd like me to go away?

JACOB: I see the hunger in you. Let us celebrate it by me giving you the soup. And you swear the birthright is mine.

ESAU: I swear, I swear, now let me eat and stop all this. I don't want to ever hear any more about it, do you understand me?

JACOB: Here, eat. (*He eats.*) Good?

ESAU: Yes, thanks, very good.

JACOB: You just sold me your birthright for a bowl of soup

ESAU: You were robbed.

Scene 2

REBECCA: Jacob, your father is dying, go and receive his blessing

JACOB: Yes mother

REBECCA: But I want you to go to him as Esau, your brother, so that you receive his blessing instead. It's bound to be worth more than your own, for Esau is the first-born and your father loves him better than he does you, Jacob.

JACOB: He loves him because he likes the venison he brings home for him to eat.

REBECCA: He has sent him off now for some. But you go and get a goat from the yard and I'll cook it in venison juice so that he won't notice. He's so old and ill that he can't really taste anything.

JACOB: But mother, do you believe a man can gain anything from a blessing intended for another man? Isn't it just like a stolen kiss. The love still belongs to the rightful owner.

REBECCA: This isn't a stolen kiss. This is a stolen maidenhead and whoever took it will always have taken it.

JACOB: But when I go in to my father he will know it is me and not Esau. Esau hasn't washed for ten years and besides he is a hairy man and I am a smooth man

REBECCA: Put on Esau's fur coat, it will provide the smell and the hairiness.

JACOB: Is my father so blind? Can he speak to give a blessing?

REBECCA: If he can't I'll move his lips for him and whisper the words into his mouth and you will kneel there and hold his hand and say, Yes Father

JACOB: You've gone insane. Why are you so full of hate? Who do you hate so much that you set son against son, and betray your dying husband?

REBECCA: (*Slaps his face.*) You are a fool. If I love or hate is no-one's concern, least of all yours. You are weak and sentimental. Also a coward. You talk of hate but you are incapable of love or hate. You are entirely selfish. You'd rob any one of us to get your way.

JACOB: I know, I know. I was just curious about you, mother. Your heart seems so shrivelled up, your hands are like claws, your eyes show nothing but greed. You're totally sexless. You have become a man. You're the kind of mother who if all her babies were starving she'd slice off bits of her legs until there was none left, then she'd feed all her little darlings the one to the other leaving one, the strongest, to survive. And through it she'd shed no tears, only sweat, and of course blood.

REBECCA: And what's wrong with that?

JACOB: There would be no point. Because with a mother like that the survivor would end up killing himself anyway.

REBECCA: And will you kill yourself when I've fed you?

JACOB: No, but only because I have inherited cowardice from my father.

REBECCA: Good, That's marvellous. Now go and find a goat

JACOB: Yes, mother.

Scene 3

JACOB: Here I am Father

ISAAC: Who is it?

JACOB: Esau, your first born. Eat this game, Father, that I have prepared for you

ISAAC: It is Jacob's voice

JACOB: No Father. (*Kisses him.*) It is I, Esau.

ISAAC: Yes. (*Feels his hands with fur gloves on.*) Esau my first-born, smells like a wild field blessed by God.

JACOB: Eat, Father.

Spoons the food into ISAAC's mouth, most of it falls back out.

Wine Father

ISAAC drinks from the cup JACOB holds.

Now may I receive your blessing?

ISAAC: God give you the fat of the land, the plenty of corn, and wine, the dew from the skies, and may all nations bow to you, and thy mother's sons bow to you. Cursed be he that curses you, blessed be he that blesses you.

ESAU comes in.

JACOB leaves.

Who is this?

ESAU: I have brought venison for you, Father

ISAAC: But I have just eaten it. Is that Esau?

ESAU: Yes, Father

ISAAC: Then I have just given your blessing to your brother. He has tricked me

ESAU: O Father, Father! Bless me too!

ISAAC: There is nothing left to give you as a blessing. I have given him dominion over you, you will bow to him. And I have given him wealth and plenty to go with it, And wine.

ESAU: Is there nothing left for me?

ISAAC: Do you think I would have held back anything from you in your blessing. I gave it all to you – to him.

ESAU: Oh Father, Father. Have you only one blessing?

ISAAC: Draw near to me. You shall have the sky for your roof and the earth for your floor. You shall live by arms and serve your brother with them until one day when you shall throw off his yoke and be free. That's all I can do. Now Esau, give me wine to drink. Pour it into my mouth Esau. I am your father. My life it isn't long. This is all the blessing I have for you.

ESAU: My blessing shall be a curse unto him that stole it. And perhaps even I shall kill him.

ISAAC: More wine Rebecca!

Scene 4

REBECCA: Jacob, you'd better run, you'd better get away. Your hairy brother wants to kill you because of what you have done

JACOB: But I don't want to run away. I want, in fact, to take me a wife

REBECCA: A wife. You'll not take one of these daughters of the land, these Canaanites. You'll go to my brother and get a wife there, you'll go into exile to Padan-Aram to get you a wife; Babylonia, Mesopotamia, Amoritia, Assyria; You'll go to Haran; to the land of Mari; to the city of Ur will you go to get thee a wife.

JACOB: That far?

REBECCA: Yes

JACOB: A foreign wife? Well, well, well.

REBECCA: But a kinswoman nevertheless

JACOB: Whatever will become of me?

REBECCA: You should have thought of that earlier

JACOB: Yes mother I should have. But somehow I don't mind. Think how exotic she'll be. I'll never be bored. I'll be enchanted with her little ways. It's not as if she'll be a monster with two heads or three breasts. She won't be half woman, half horse. I won't have to ride her bareback in the forest all night screaming will I mother, do you think? She won't be mad or bad. And if heaven permits it and time allows, I'll learn her language for myself and be all the wiser for it, be all the more a man of the world, all the more useful to myself and others, for it won't I? What a lad I'll be. They'll all want me and I'll want them

REBECCA: Go on now Jacob before I lose both my sons on one day

JACOB: I'll go now mother. Tell Esau to cool off, And tell my father Isaac I am sorry I couldn't stay for his funeral. And you mother most of all, I know you'll need comforting in the troubled times ahead, and widowed with Esau only for a son, your lot won't be very grand. Think of me though, at night in the blackness, let's hope neither of us gets lost

Scene 5

JACOB alone out in the desert's blackness.

JACOB: What darkness, I have never seen darkness like it before. I am asleep dreaming and yet I am awake and speaking to myself in this nothingness. My voice is alone calling out to me and yet I am asleep dreaming. And though I am asleep dreaming I cannot believe what I see.

For though I put my head on a stone because I am the
fugitive out in the blackness fleeing from my wronged
brother whose rage wants to kill me, though I am the
thief and the liar with my head on a stone, I am truly
seeing great things! For from my poor head stretches up
a great ladder to the stars but I am not climbing on it,
I am lying in the dust like the fugitive. Instead, climbing
on the ladder are angels, yes the true angels of the Lord
and they are climbing up and climbing down towards me
and away from me and I am not afraid and I am on my
back alone and unafraid. Some men would be lonely out
here running as I am. But I am empty like a cup, I feel
nothing. Instead I dream. I will surely never wake up.
The weight of this celestial ladder presses me down to
the earth so that I can never move again. I will remain
here dreaming forever. This is a strange place and I have
stumbled here by accident. This is not a place where
men have ever been or will ever go, only me. This is
God's place, and I didn't know it.

This is a dreadful place. Look, the Lord God calls out to
me; Jacob, Jacob, sayeth the Lord, I am with thee and
I will multiply thee as the dust you sleep in, your seed
will fill the earth. I am the God of your father Isaac and
his father Abraham, but it is you I shall follow wherever
you go on this earth. If you run this way or that, will you
do your mother's bidding and find her niece, will you be
in exile and marry some strange girl who bears your
blood in her – I shall be with you, I will lay it all at your
feet, I will open wombs for your seed. I will give you
this girl with the strange voice, I will lead you abroad
into the hands of a cunning father, but it is you who will
cheat him.

Is this the Lord God speaking? I am laughing, I can hear
my voice laughing but these are things I do not know.
My grandmother laughed when my father was conceived.
I will perhaps laugh too… Am I an imbecile? Is God

with me? Is He perhaps an imbecile? This is a dreadful place. God's voice has stopped, mine can begin again. Who am I? Jacob. I am less than my brother Esau; though he is dull minded, I am duller. I am the laughing stock. I wore his smell to cheat my father. They are still laughing now. I am a dog with his master's birthright in his mouth. God is with me. I am the biggest fool who has ever lived. Cain dealt in blood whereas I served up some soup. The hairy man should have killed me but now I will make a covenant with God. He will follow me in my adventures and I will – I will... God! Lord! Lord! I will kneel here in your spot, your dreadful spot. I will build you an altar out of my pillow and Lord I will, if you give me food and clothes, and Lord if you lead me back in peace to my father's house one day, why then Lord you shall be the Lord my God – and I shall give you a tenth of any profits, Lord

AN ANGEL: Hello Jacob, sleeping down there in the blackness. See me on top of my ladder? I am the Lord God, God of Hosts, Lord of Gods. My kingdom stretches as far as far can be, from the oars of the Phoenecians in the west to the gutter of Ur, the mighty city of cities, in the east, I am the drop of water for each, I am the dew in the sky falling upon your toes Jacob, I am the God, no less, of Abraham your grandfather. Kneel and tremble

JACOB: Yes, I've heard of you, we call you the God of sheep, the bucket and the well. 'Old Pickaxe' my dad calls you, and my dear dear mother, a beauty in her day but now a bitter herb, uses you to curse her husband my father. But only yesterday in fact she said aloud; God curse God! she said, and ground her great white teeth together in her head. And I thought to myself; Ma, that's hardly possible

ANGEL: Yes Jacob Great things, great things indeed. You have made a fine fellow of yourself. And now I shall sing my song to you out of the depths of my sorrow. I've brought you this far Jacob, but I don't know what to do with you. I wish I could take you down in my bed to dream my dreams with me, or to sleep and sleep away forever, never to return. How can I possibly have anything to say to you Jacob? May your seed be like dust, may you turn this way and that, to left and to right. And whichever way you do turn Jacob, there shall I be, above you and below you. I shall take you there and bring you back. Your journey shall be long and yet it is the piece of dirt you now lie upon that I shall give to you and your generations. This is my blessing Jacob and by God I won't leave you until I have done these things

JACOB: (*Awakes.*) This is surely God's place I am in and didn't know it. So dreadful a place. The God of my father leads me here and indeed if he does all he says and my seed is scattered like dust and my way is turned from east to west and from west to east, then indeed if he bringeth me back to my father's land, to my home then shall He be the Lord my God.

I shall write this dream. I shall write it in the moonlight. All honour to thee my drunken father. All success to thee scheming mother, All peace to thee murdering brother. All glory to thee God of gods who sought me out on my pillow of stone. Oh great God of the wilderness. Oh secret God who reveals himself to me. Oh singing God, your song is singing itself in my ears, still singing and ringing, Singing God. In this place, the place of the dread Lord, this dark place, I shall set up an altar to thee Great Singing God. Behold it shall be my little stony pillow.

Scene 6

GOD and LUCIFER.

GOD: And so it is, Lucifer, with the sons of men. Do you see what kind of a God they have, singing songs to them in the dessert? Oh if I had a song to sing do they really think I would sing it to them?

LUCIFER: Then it wasn't you?

GOD: No, it was you

LUCIFER: Me? Does this mean you don't like them?

GOD: I didn't say that

LUCIFER: It is very easy after all to dislike them for their evil-doing

GOD: Well yes

LUCIFER: And for their ridiculous pride

GOD: Yes, of course

LUCIFER: Or just for their meanness and stupidity, they really are quite disgusting

GOD: Disgusting yes, of course

LUCIFER: But my point is that it is just as ridiculous to be a misanthrope

GOD: Precisely, just as ridiculous to be a misanthrope

LUCIFER: It is ridiculous, ugly and strangely contemptible

GOD: Yes it is

LUCIFER: Why is that?

GOD: That is because to be a misanthrope involves all the sins of pride and hypocrisy and the lack of charity that, seen in other men, provokes the misanthropy in the first place; And because the only difference between a misanthrope and other men is that he cannot see that there isn't one.

LUCIFER: Yes, that's interesting, its interesting because –

GOD: Dammit, I'm tired of all this. Listen, it's spring, the birdies are singing although the sun's not yet up. It's warm, after having been cold all winter. Don't you see I'm in a different mood now? Frankly I'm like two different people. I don't think that's necessarily something to be ashamed of do you?

LUCIFER: No. But now I'm all confused. You say all of a sudden that these big questions don't matter. Then you ask me for an opinion on something quite trivial, as to whether it matters to be like two different people. It makes me tired. I feel as if I am floating. Don't you really care about anything?

GOD: When it's spring I see different possibilities

LUCIFER: Such as?

GOD: Such as ? Love I suppose.

LUCIFER: You think there is hope of love in the spring?

GOD: Yes, hope of love in the spring. Then comes summer, lying in that rowing boat hearing that clunk clunk of the water and the oars that men like so much because it reminds them of the womb, then autumn and fingering the buttons on each other's coats in the crisp cold afternoon light, then winter, you are both obscured by scarves. It's all so easy to imagine, the start and the finish. But now I don't think about any of that I just feel a joyous kind of thrill, the excitement of love

LUCIFER: You think about her now, Mary the object of your love?

GOD: Yes, her shy smile, the hands folded in front of her, her top lip

LUCIFER: Will you go to see her?

GOD: It's likely I shall move across the Shadows of the deep. But at the same time I am afraid. Afraid I might love her too much. The journey fills me with terror, moving across the face of the waters. Then the horror of being in two places at the same time. So lonely.

Scene 7

JACOB arrives at Padan-Aram, the well of Haran. Some men are watering their sheep.

JACOB: Who is that woman, friend?

BROTHER: She is our sister, Rachel. She looks after us, gives us comfort when our father neglects us, gives us alibis when we sneak away at night; She holds us in her arms when we are afraid

JACOB: Would you try to stop me if I tried to marry her?

BROTHER: Not if you are a good man

JACOB: And you can only tell that from what I can see in your sister, isn't that correct?

BROTHER: That is correct

JACOB: Well, I see in her that she is a protector of children in the form of her brothers, that she is therefore brave and able to overlook her own fears in the service of others. She is therefore both noble and humble. I see in her demeanour that while she stands perfectly erect so that her beauty is instantly noticeable, her hands are folded before her and her eyes are peaceful and shy; from that I can see that she has an inner life which is for her more important than any other accomplishments or gifts of God that she may possess. I see also from her complete patience in attending to her brothers that she cares little, or knows not how to care for, her own life and is content in each moment as it presents itself to her.

BROTHER: You have told me about my sister that is dearer to me than all people on earth. She is my mother, my teacher, my friend, my all. She teaches me how to think and to speak, to hold my tongue, to fight, to love, to be a man. She protected me from the dark when I was a child, and shields me from the light now I am a man. You wish to take her from us?

JACOB: I am the son of a well digger, the genius of the pump and the bucket and the son of your kinswoman. I am also not a drunkard but a quiet man of some cunning, and although I have only petty ambition myself, the Gods have great things planned for me

BROTHER: Are you a thief?

JACOB: No, I open my hands and God showers gifts into them. But to win your sister I would be willing to renounce this clear advantage I have over others and work. Yes, go and tell your father I will labour seven years for him if at the end of it this girl will be my wife

BROTHER: Is there a message I should give her that you hope may win her approval of this idea?

JACOB: Yes, tell her I have dreamt about God. He descended a ladder to me

RACHEL: (*Approaches.*) Who is this?

BROTHER: This is our kinsman

RACHEL: Can you roll away the stone of the well so that I can water my father's sheep?

JACOB: Yes.

RACHEL: Why are you staring?

JACOB kisses the earth before her feet.

Scene 8

GOD: Well, my fairy, how have you dealt with that great pair of swindlers, Jacob and Laban his father-in-law?

LUCIFER: First Jacob worked seven toilsome years to win Rachel. This didn't matter to him for although by instinct he found work to be a loathsome occupation, the years flew by on account of the marvellous prize awaiting him.

GOD: Good, good. And then on the wedding night...?

LUCIFER: Laban sent his other daughter Leah into Jacob's tent instead of Rachel

JACOB: What hast though done? I served seven years for Rachel, not for Leah

LABAN: But that is not the tradition in our country. The eldest daughter must marry first.

JACOB: Well, you might have told me that seven years ago!

LABAN: Didn't I mention it?

LUCIFER: So Jacob served another seven years to get Rachel, but Lo and Behold! – Rachel was barren.

JACOB emerges from RACHEL's tent.

LABAN: Sorry about that. You'll have to fructify her maid instead.

JACOB: Her maid?

LABAN: (*Presents her.*) Bilhah

JACOB returns towards the tent with BILHAH.

Not forgetting Leah, of course.

JACOB: No, right. (*Goes inside the tent.*)

LUCIFER: So while Leah bore Jacob sons, and Rachel's maid bore him a son, Rachel prayed unto the Lord

GOD: And what did I decide?

RACHEL: I have raised up my voice to the Lord and he hath given me a son

JACOB: Oh good. What shall we call him?

RACHEL: (*Running out of names.*) ...Dan?

GOD: That's very nice

LUCIFER: Meanwhile Rachel's maid also conceived him another son.

JACOB looks towards one of the tents.

RACHEL: With great wrestlings I have wrestled with my sister, and I have prevailed

JACOB: Another son?

RACHEL: Napthali

GOD: It's going very well, good my bird

LUCIFER: You think Jacob might be tired?

LEAH: Jacob, I have left off conceiving

JACOB: Ah...

LEAH: So here is my maid Zilpah

JACOB: Right. Thanks.

LUCIFER: ...and Zilpah bare him two sons. And Leah was happy for all the sons she, and her maid, had borne Jacob. Now it came to pass that Leah's son Reuben went into the fields in the days of the wheat harvest and collected the narcotic flowers, Mandrakes, to which Rachel was partial;

RACHEL: Leah, give me of your son's mandrakes, I pray thee.

LEAH: Huh! Not likely! Do you think it a small matter that you took my husband from me?

RACHEL: *Your* husband?

LEAH: And would you now take my son's mandrakes?

RACHEL: Give me the mandrakes and Jacob can sleep with you tonight even though its my turn

LEAH: Done.

JACOB approaches, weary from his labours. He heads towards RACHEL's tent but...

Thou must come in to me tonight, for I have hired thee with my son's mandrakes

LUCIFER: And she bare him another son, ...and another. And a daughter.

LEAH: Surely he will live with me now

LUCIFER: But you in your wisdom, Lord

GOD smiles.

hearkened unto the pleas of Rachel and opened her womb and...

GOD: She bore him another son?

LUCIFER: Joseph.

RACHEL: God hath taken away my reproach.

LUCIFER: And at this point Jacob went unto Laban and said;

JACOB: I'm tired from my labours of fourteen years. I have at least twelve sons. I would like to go home now if you wouldn't mind, with my sons and my wives.

LABAN: And their maids.

JACOB: And their maids

LUCIFER: And thus were begun the twelve tribes of Israel, thy chosen people Lord

GOD: Very good. Very Good! (*Shakes his head and laughs.*)

Scene 9

GOD: And was Jacob well paid on his departure for his 14 years of labours?

LUCIFER: Well, the deal was that he should take as payment the spotted and the speckled goats and the brown sheep from Laban's greatly increased flock, but Laban swindled him by removing all these beforehand.

GOD: Oh dear

LUCIFER: Not to worry, Jacob swindled him back again by using a cunning magic trick to make all the sheep conceive brown lambs, and all the goats conceive spotted kids, and the rest he painted with a white stick and indeed he ended up with most of Laban's cattle, for truly, with the Grace of God, Jacob was the master swindler of the two

JACOB: (*To RACHEL.*) The angel of the Lord appeared to me and said 'paint this little man's sheep and take the lot, for I see what he hath done to thee, changing thy wages ten times and so on.' So, Rachel, the Lord has taken away thy father's cattle and given them to me. Amen.

RACHEL: For my part by the grace of God, I took these pictures off the wall.

JACOB: Good. Now where did I park that camel?

End of Act Two.

ACT THREE

Scene 1

LUCIFER: Why are You sad, Oh Lord God of Hosts?

GOD: I am sad because all my creations are inferior. See them breaking and bowing under the weight of their imperfections. I am the author of the Vale of Tears. Last night I sat alone on a leaf and wept.

LUCIFER: But the Vale of Tears would have flourished if You had lived there all alone

GOD: What? Shall God live in a garden? Shall I pass across the waters like a boat? Shall I shoot across the stars like a burnt rock? Shall I swim in the sea like a fish? Or jump at the sun at dusk from the silver rivers? Shall I roll down the mountains like an ant? And sing in the sky, being a lark? And hoot in the dark like an owl? Do I suppose myself to be a bison God, to trample and roll my plains, the lonesome iron hoof, dancing in the dust?

I am the god of decay and of drowning! The God of the rat and the quiet grave! The God of disaster! Come to me with your dead, I am the God of the Dead, come to me with your broken wars, and your history! I have been broken in your wars and I sleep in your history as you do!

LUCIFER: Doesn't Man mock at Your decay, making himself a god of destruction?

GOD: Yes, he builds, then he destroys

LUCIFER: And doesn't he fear the rat and despise the quiet grave?

GOD: There are peaceful tombs left, I have seen them

LUCIFER: But he won't sleep alongside the dead. And he is proud of his little life

GOD: I can wait for him

GOD's giant soul soars above.

What is this little voice beside me? Is it you Michael? Is it you Gabriel? Is it you Lucifer? What is it you are saying? Speak up. You sound so far away as in a dream! It's you Lucifer, I know you by your light. Whose light is it? Did I give it to you?

LUCIFER: This is the light You gave me

GOD: Does it illumine my darkness Lucifer?

LUCIFER: I know not

GOD: And if I take it from you will I lose my darkness, will you take my darkness away from Me?

LUCIFER: I know not

GOD: I have created light and so drawn the bounds of darkness. Where will my soul sleep in those days? That light shines making some of my darkness pale, Some of my darkness dark, Some of my sleeping dream, Some of my sleeping sleep.

And in those days when you have taken my darkness, I will have only the light. Where will I be then?

LUCIFER: You will cease to exist. You will be in the imaginations of men

GOD: You will plant my darkness there, in the minds of men, beside me like a weed.

LUCIFER: Will I die when I take Your darkness?

GOD: No

LUCIFER: Will you take back your darkness from the imaginations of men?

GOD: I will, but not before they have banished both Me *and* my darkness from their imaginations. And when they do

35

I will have it back, then I will reign in glory over them and they won't know it. This is the prophesy of the Lord!

LUCIFER: Praise be To God! (*Pause.*) Are they fools, these men?

GOD: Yes Lucifer they are

LUCIFER: What about the evil you do to them?

GOD: Yes Lucifer. Disease and disaster, pain and suffering. When there isn't enough meat or bread, when there isn't enough water, when something accidentally falls on someone's head, When they all die, Death.

Can you imagine the genius that went into that idea? When out of the continuance of My existence, I gave birth to Death

O God Help Me! (*He kneels.*) If there is anyone, please forgive Me!

Gets up.

You see, if there wasn't a God I would have to invent one.

In fact some men invent gods above Me, and other gods above them, an endless pyramid of appeal across the spheres. Sometimes I allow Myself the luxury of believing there is a God above Me. But most of the time I am brave enough to be, …an agnostic. I rule out nothing. How could anyone know?

LUCIFER: Aren't you omniscient?

GOD: I don't know

Scene 2

LUCIFER: Send your son to save them

GOD: I have no son. Can a tree send a crocus to feed the birds? Your thoughts are obscure

LUCIFER: He can be a blood sacrifice to pay for their sins

GOD: Pay whom?

LUCIFER: Pay you

GOD: How rich in blood I would be if only I had a son!

LUCIFER: Make yourself your own son

GOD: Split myself in two?

LUCIFER: You are already two

GOD: To those who can't count to one

LUCIFER: Among them I name myself. I refer to Your secret life; away from me, invisible to me Your spirit wanders the face of the Universe, while You pretend to stay here upon this burning isle with me.

Send Your son, but if you have none go Yourself. If You cannot go Yourself amongst them, make Yourself a man like them. You the father of man can become the son of man, the son of fear, the son of death ,the son of ignorance

GOD: If I go amongst them they will kill me as they kill each other. Must I suffer at their hands? Shall *I* also fear my death

LUCIFER: You can share love with them

GOD: But will I love them as I love her? I think of her in her perfection, and of my misery for her sake, and I conclude that all that could have gone right has gone right, and all that could have gone wrong has gone wrong. Mary. Sometimes when I search in her for the key to her brightness I find only the dark.

Lucifer, there is a limpet at the bottom of a clear pool, clinging in fear and shadows. Who put it there?

LUCIFER: You don't know?

GOD: You fiend! Nobody knows!

LUCIFER: And who is this limpet?

GOD: You don't know?

LUCIFER: No, my Lord

GOD: It's Me, my friend, it's Me.

Scene 3

GABRIEL: Mary, you are to have a son. You will call him Jesus, he is the son of God

MARY: But how? I am a virgin

GABRIEL: God has projected His seed into you by sheer willpower.

MARY: It's a pity I didn't even know about it.

GABRIEL: Mary, please, I'm just the messenger

MARY: He never allowed Himself to touch me. Now I am to look after His son

GABRIEL: Don't you want His child?

MARY: Of course I do. But I wanted so many things. This is the last I'll ever hear of Him. I will pray in vain, I will wait in vain. I am the forlorn one, the forgotten one, the rejected one. I am the object of divine love and will spend all my days in futile sorrow. My life is not a life to live but to regret, always in the shadow of my misery. I have seen the face of God and He was no god, I have known a lover and he was no lover. I'm no fool. This son of mine, this son of God, he will not be a man, he will not live, he will die. He is the stillborn son of our stillborn love. Get out of my sight Gabriel, you sicken me to my soul; so beautiful but yet not God, not my love, a messenger, a stand-in, a representative, nothing in yourself. You are like me, what my life will be. Mother to a son who is no son, of no father, the orphan in my womb. He is a bastard, I am a whore, and my husband is a cuckold. You see I weep at his conception, shall no doubt cry out at his birth, and, I fear, live to shed tears at his death. How will anyone endure it? This exile from my love, in pain and misery? Only one thing will keep me alive.

GABRIEL: God has said His great love makes this necessary

MARY: Tell him only my great love makes it possible

Scene 4

JOSEPH: What is it like, Mary, to be with someone so much older than yourself? I've sometimes wondered, just out of curiosity

MARY: Oh, well, I don't really think about it

JOSEPH: It occurred to me though, that there is one important difference between our two positions. Shall I annoy you by telling you what it is?

MARY: Annoy me

JOSEPH: It's a riddle. Something that I know but you can only guess. What is it?

MARY: I don't know, what is it?

JOSEPH: I *know* what it's like to be twenty, but you can only guess at what it's like to be thirty three.

MARY: That's true

JOSEPH: Clever isn't it?

MARY: Yes

JOSEPH: Why do you look so sad Mary? I'm only teasing you

MARY: I'm sorry, but I *don't* guess at what it's like to be thirty three because I find it painful

JOSEPH: Why is it painful Mary?

MARY: I can't imagine myself reaching that age. I see only death.

JOSEPH: My darling. Here's me chattering away like a fool and you announce this darkness within you

MARY: I'm sorry Joseph

JOSEPH: Do you really mean it, that you have no hope?

MARY: Yes.

JOSEPH: Don't you want to live?

MARY: No. Oh don't look so sad.

JOSEPH: I am sad, but I am also thinking; why do you have me then? I think there must be a reason; You have chosen me as an emblem of your despair. For I am that which you never expect to be. All the better because of my happy nature, I am the bitterer memento mori. Should I wear black do you think and carry an axe; Or should I dance with bells?

MARY: You should dance with bells

JOSEPH: Alright. But should I sing? Or should I bend over in prayer like this – Oh God, O Cruel One, Send us a sign! Send us an angel to prove Your goodness Lord! And if you can't send us an angel, send us an arch angel, and if you cant send us an archangel send us your sister, and if she won't come then you'd better come yourself, because dammit Lord we need some cheering up. Look at this poor girl, Mary! She's beautiful, she's intelligent, from a good family, and a nice town, she's well married certainly! But is she happy? Look at the long face on her Lord. There's only one thing for it, by God, send us your jester!

MARY: His jester? Do you think He will?

JOSEPH: Oh yes, of course he will. And do you know what he'll do when he gets here? He'll abolish religion. Yes, that's the first thing he'll do. Then he'll do something about all this washing that goes on

MARY: Washing?

JOSEPH: Yes, haven't you noticed how people are washing all the time?

MARY: People *are* very clean

JOSEPH: Clean? Washing has lost all meaning! He'll restore significance to washing, and return dirt to its proper place. Then they'll kill him

MARY: Joseph, don't. Who will?

JOSEPH: Who will what?

MARY: Kill God's jester

JOSEPH: Did I say kill him? Oh well, of course they will kill him. They'll jump on him and flatten him, put words in his mouth, and choke him with them. But the question is; Would this cheer you up at all? Would it give you the hope you so sorely lack?

MARY: No Joseph

JOSEPH: No, but why?

MARY: It would be sad

JOSEPH: Sad, yes. But happy-sad, don't you think?

MARY: Possibly, if he was a good jester

JOSEPH: That's it! It's a question of quality. *Nous le reconnaitrons à ses blagues*

MARY: And what then?

JOSEPH: Well, we have the wind

MARY: Yes

JOSEPH: And

MARY: Yes

JOSEPH: And the seven seas

MARY: But we're nowhere near the sea

JOSEPH: You're never far from the sea

MARY: And of course you are frightened by the sea

JOSEPH: *Of course* I am frightened by the sea

End of Act Three.

ACT FOUR

Scene 1

LUCIFER: God looked at me and said; When the brightness
of your eye declines, what darkness will be there

We take up the action where Captain Eddie is locked in
combat with his bowels in the labour ward... This is
called Dream of the birth of God –

MARY, JOSEPH, a crib and a DONKEY and ATTENDANTS.

Enter NURSE Goodwoman.

NURSE: God forgive yez all
    Just one more push
    And his old bald head
    Will be showing. Just
    Hold me darling 'till I squeeze him
    Out

DONKEY: What will we call him, Mrs Spam?

MRS SPAM: Mrs Bacon is a name I've always liked. In fact
they called me something similar when I was born

A SPY: What kind of name is that for the son of Mr Freedom's
dad, the Almighty?

A MOCKER: Infinite Keech, Miss jelly jowls, Yellow guts,
Miss universe

A SPY: The Germ

A MOCKER: Back-to-the-womb

A SPY: Chief Broken Canoe

A MOCKER: Master shot-in-the-dark, Pig in a poke, Cock
in a bag

NURSE: Ask the mother what she thinks

DONKEY: She isn't thinking right now, she's being

NURSE: Then I've got a little nickname I call him already, I call him the naughty little man

A SPY: He's a bloody yobboe

DONKEY: Let him be born first, bless him!

A MOCKER: Keratoid, the Rhino

A SPY: Jack Ketch, Daddy's little helper

A MOCKER: The mosquito

A SPY: Easy Joe Quickfinger, Maker of Heaven and Earth

A MOCKER: Mr Electricity

A SPY: The Mouse

A MOCKER: Beautiful Young Woman With Mercy

A SPY: Mr Smith, the virgin Queen

A MOCKER: Mr Best – the best!

A SPY: Hail Mary, after his mum

DONKEY: Words are failing us, we'll have to go for something small

A MOCKER: Tight fist

A SPY: Little nut, the acorn

DONKEY: Mike

NURSE: Pete

DONKEY: John

A SPY: God.

NURSE: OK, God it is, but it doesn't look like we've got the best of all possible names

DONKEY: We'll see how he turns out, and if he's better than we expected we'll look for something more suitable

NURSE: Now all together... Push! Pull! Push! Pull! That's it girls!

They all push and pull at one of NURSE's buttocks in a nice rhythm.

MR WHEELWRIGHT: (*The inventor of the wheel.*) But how long can this go on for before we produce anything? You're only the midwife!

NURSE: Take hold of that buttock Mr Wheelwright and PULL! Never you mind your scientific intrusions into the secrets of the universe!

JESUS: While I was struggling to be born, many scenes were being acted out around me. In my sleep I painted tales of Freedom on the cave walls of my ancient memory, renewing the old clear pictures now being erased as I slipped by. I scribbled madly, racing against the new enemy, Time. Streams of air passed over dim green pools where a giant fish basked in the reeds, and it whispered to me that it was the prince of Darkness and that it too was waiting to be born. I pushed on my way and saw great generals marching on a path across the void, leading hosts of frogs and crickets riding the backs of donkeys; 'we are émigrés and other visitors,' they said, 'all going to a celestial tea' and I rowed my small wooden boat across the puffy blue sky with its chain dragging in the tree tops, and looking down to see the rivers and streams motioning down below, flowing inland from the sea, promising to return when Joy is done and labour is begun

MR WHEELWRIGHT: I know nursie, I know, but my piles are hurting me, I can hardly speak for them!

A MOCKER: The window is open Jack Wheelright my old friend

MR WHEELWRIGHT: That doesn't mean I *have* to jump does it?

A MOCKER: What a man of many vices you are! And a coward to boot!

A SPY: Jack the Robber! – Jesus!

Scene 2

JESUS: (*As a baby.*) For the days that followed I was a cabbage, a page in a book, a field of grass, then God himself, and finally even a bucket of water. In all these manifestations I had wisdom to impart to the world, apart from the day when I was in fact the world itself, and on that day I had no wisdom at all to impart to no-one except to an old cow in a field who asked me the way to Shannon airport at which I must confess I pointed her off in the wrong way altogether, but then that is the way of the world is it not?

Hey! Didn't you hear me calling out there from my high-chair?

A SPY: Heard nothing else.

A MOCKER: And good luck to you!

A SPY: Not a peep out of the others

A MOCKER: You've struck them dumb with your few words and your gurgling

A SPY: Well Mr Novelty, how's the reincarnation going?

JESUS: I was a cricket stump last week

A MOCKER: Keep them guessing

A SPY: What is that infernal racket?

JESUS: That's my horse running about upstairs. I don't know what the burglars think of him but he scares the life out of me!

A SPY: You can't be too careful

JESUS: I've only been alive six weeks and its all bad memories so far. I'd like to put it all behind me

A MOCKER: Look to the future

A SPY: That's right

A MOCKER: I've been wondering Mr Freedom, Is change possible?

JESUS: (*Mutters to himself.*) Is it necessary, that's what I wonder. Oh the pain! Let me sleep

A MOCKER: Mr Freedom likes his nap doesn't he?

Enter a great COMMUNICATOR.

COMMUNICATOR: Ah Mr Liberty! Step right this way. A host of independent young minds awaits you. They're deciding on their questions, they'd like to ask you, right now as we speak

JESUS: God rot them

MRS SPAM: Set up the drinks there Joe, You know what they say; If you're going to fall its not a long way down.

JESUS: (*Raises his glass.*) My health

A MOCKER: What's today's invention O poet?

JESUS: It is Reconciliation

A MOCKER: Impossible

JESUS: Man's destiny depends on it

A SPY: Who should he reconcile himself with?

JESUS: His neighbour, his enemy, his loved ones, his most feared adversary

A MOCKER: (*With an air of incredulity.*) You mean people he doesn't like??

JESUS: Yes

A SPY: People who oppose his every effort? Who make
death and failure a certainty, who bring destruction and
misery upon mankind and shame upon the spirit? Whose
lust for vengeance counts no cost in blood and disaster,
those beasts who pile the bones of their victims like a
child does shells on a beach? Those fiends who mock
and laugh at the anguish of their victims? Those enemies
of reconciliation, you would try to reconcile with those?
What if they refuse?

JESUS: I sometimes find being alive in this world of men
akin to standing on a small coin; You cannot push or
strain against its edges for there are none, you are on a
disk. You push at the air and eventually you fall off.
Finally of course, falling off is a relief

A SPY: You're right. How can a man reform humanity in
the span of seventy years? You should ask your father for
more time, perhaps a thousand or two?

JESUS: All that time to be the butt of their corruption?
I know their game; I'd be unrecognisable by the end of
it. They'd turn me from thief to lover to tyrant and then
when you'd think no further indignity was possible, –
they'd make me their buddy.

A SPY: Very unpleasant

Re-enter the COMMUNICATOR.

COMMUNICATOR: Who's that baby waving? Is it…? Is
it…? Do I have the pleasure of… Young Mr Freedom?
(*He shakes his hand vigorously, too vigorously.*) Welcome
again Sir, I am here to tell you that you are sent to us as
a Great Rebel, leader of the big rebellion. What a fine
man!

JESUS: To rebel against what, may I enquire?

48

COMMUNICATOR: Can't you see? Isn't it obvious. Why, against Man, the World, and Slavery. Against the burden of free will, Against suffering and persecution, and countless governments, (a list will be supplied.), if not all of them, Against service stations, the motor car, civil liberties, prejudice, Humanity itself and her cruelty, The vitality of the aeroplane

LADY COUNCILLOR: (*His assistant.*) And later there's our Feast of Fools, in which we eat anyone who dares to mock us

A MOCKER: It's working very well, I think he's impressed

LADY COUNCILLOR: (*Encouraged by the MOCKER's opinion of how things are going.*) Yes, Baby Jesus, look into the Great Communicator's eyes, tell us what you see

JESUS: The light of Justice, flickering on and off

A SPY: Ah Mr Pork Sausage, born again at last

LADY COUNCILLOR: (*Resigned and happy.*) It's a child's world isn't it

COMMUNICATOR: Well what do you think of the assembled company, the younger generation, they're all yours and at your service! All of them non-smokers, equipt with take-it-with-you mobile dance stations, what do you think? The subculture, the beat, beat, beat, devil-may-take-the-hindmost, technobabble, hip-hop Fuck You megaculture, what do you think?

JESUS: It seems there's no getting away from it

COMMUNICATOR: They're all on your side, Mr Freedom!

JESUS: Thank them, send them my apologies.

LADY COUNCILLOR: They don't take no for an answer. I thought our next port of call could be a very interesting wharfside warehouse middle-of-no-where location pirouetting party with vol-au-vents cocktails and an anti education seminar with drinkies and a dance. I have the programme with seventeen-colour printing in a van outside – it's injectable directly into your little brain, no need to read it.

JESUS: Wasn't that wharf once my father's house?

LADY COUNCILLOR: You mean your uncle, the lovely Lord Commerce? He's still very much in evidence, don't worry, only now he wears Khaki shorts and pretends to be a male prostitute. They call him Kneeling Nigel. He judges our poetry competitions.

A SPY: But isn't he illiterate due to his lazy eye?

LADY COUNCILLOR: We don't look at it that way – We think of him as having one *busy* eye

COMMUNICATOR: May I say something Mr Freedom?

JESUS: Call me Jim

COMMUNICATOR: Jim – We are all made in your image. We have been admiring your portrait for decades.

JESUS: Do you want my honest opinion?

COMMUNICATOR: *Natürlich*

JESUS: I'm very disappointed to be here

LADY COUNCILLOR: Oh I say!

JESUS: I'd rather be back in my primeval sludge with a dead fish

COMMUNICATOR: But you can lead us on to the final victory

JESUS: Victory is not a thing I am accustomed to. Let's go back to the labour ward and pull Nursie's buttocks

A MOCKER: Didn't you notice her buttocks were totally empty?

JESUS: Nevertheless they are the breasts from which succour may be given

A SPY: Won't it involve us in a heresy?

JESUS: These days Boyo, it's the only way my favourite old-style religion gets a look in.

They begin to depart severally.

LUCIFER: (*Aside, in passing.*) The Feast of Fools is where the Lord God is allowed to become man and subject his institutions to ridicule…

Scene 3

JESUS: Then from his sleep the baby wakes and cries, and then goes back again. Nothing gained or lost, another cough and a sneeze on the path to the big nowhere; when Man falters he stops and sets up tents and robs himself and slaughters his cattle with sticks. All done in the name of some strange daemon to spite the name of God my father. Man is a vainglorious little beast wrapped in self-pity.

Soon they'll all come to me asking their questions, but I'll give them no answers. I shall say to them; Behold the simpering man who says 'my people are this, my people are that, they have done this wrong and need to be punished, oh Lord', or 'Oh destiny', or 'oh history', or 'oh politics'… And I shall say; You are the man you think you are not; if you think you are the labourer, you are the foreman, if you think you are the disciple, you are the tax-collector, if you think you are a freethinkingman you are the narrow minded bigot, if you think you are of the twentieth century you are of the previous one. Are you looking forward to the future?, you should fear it. Do you think you've come a long way?, you have gone backwards. You are like the man who for years laboured in his master's vineyard and became a foreman in that vinyard and went in coloured robes and who was at last eating at his master's table displacing the old foreman and his children who are now put to work in the vineyards as he was. And while these bend under the yoke, and sweat under the sun, this man sitting at the cool table eating fruit, turns to the master and says 'why do you oppress us with this foreman who bends and sweats over us so we can hardly eat?' But the master has fled into the field, and lies prostrate under the vines. And this man at the table smiles to himself because everything has changed, 'for now', he says to himself, 'although I am still oppressed by the master and his foreman, I who worked in the fields now sit at the table. Now there is justice!'

Scene 4

A MAN, WOMAN, BABY beside a well.

JESUS: What are you doing? You are not praying are you I can tell that.

MAN: No, I'm drawing water from this well, 30ft, 60ft, 120ft 12,000ft, its so far down it scares me to even look. My arms are exhausted. My wife and baby are asleep in the shade. Now memories surge over me so that I nearly fall asleep myself

JESUS: Why don't you take a nap?

MAN: Because then the bucket would fall and I'd have to hoist it all the way back up again

JESUS: What kind of memories do you have while you do this kind of work?

MAN: What kind of memories? Memories of other wells of course! Now mister, how can I help you?

JESUS: I'm thirsty

MAN: Thought you might be. You've come to the right place then haven't you? Now get hold of that my old son and give it a few turns, that's it, while I sit down here and rest. You don't mind?

JESUS: No. We'll share the water

MAN: That's right

JESUS: So how come you are here today?

MAN: Not for fun I assure you. It's all gone wrong as you can see. I'm a trained engineer. I build roads.

JESUS: A romantic job perhaps?

MAN: Very observant. But that was once upon a time. It isn't now. The world doesn't want roads. Can't you see the world is bloody covered in them, its drowning under them, choking, suffocating, disappearing, becoming ugly and ill under them. They've sort of lost their symbolical quality, sort of lost their romantic quality

JESUS: Thanks for putting me straight

MAN: Thanks, yes. Have you any idea where that puts me? Once I would have built pathways of adventure for the soaring human spirit, – now I'm the villain who enchains and destroys. Have you any idea how that feels?

JESUS: Some. I've some idea how that feels

Scene 5

JUDAS: One question Jesus

JESUS: Yes, Judas

JUDAS: Can't we live in a world without pain and suffering? I'd like to

JESUS: That is not the nature of this world, as far as I can see

JUDAS: Can't you ask your father for this gift?

JESUS: You ask Him Judas. You ask the God you pray to for this thing.

JUDAS: How can my prayers move Him?

JESUS: What is wrong with your prayers, Judas?

JUDAS: I have no prayers. When you pray I watch over you to protect you

JESUS: Pray with me now Judas

JUDAS: I cannot. I am ashamed

JESUS: Then you pray to Him and I will watch over you

JUDAS: But my prayers are full of contradictions

JESUS: You see yourself as a cripple Judas, but you are a man, a good man. Look your God in the eye.

JUDAS: My God is not the same as your God

JESUS: You pray to your God, Judas, He will hear you

JUDAS: Jesus

JESUS: Yes my brother?

JUDAS: I don't like my God

JESUS: Do you wish you were me, Judas?

JUDAS: Yes, Lord

JESUS: We are all so alone

JUDAS: I am always looking over my shoulder at you talking with God and I end up hating myself and the God I speak to

JESUS: Are you afraid to be alone, Judas my brother?

JUDAS: It's so empty, Jesus, only me there and my hated, false God. What am I to do?

JESUS: Share my sorrow with me Judas. My God is called false and hated for his cruelty by men, and always has been and always will be

JUDAS: You are leaving us soon aren't you?

JESUS: In all my despair ahead Judas, it is you I will think of. Promise me you will think of me in your despair

JUDAS: I am poor in spirit, Lord, and cannot give nor share. I beg and steal and gape inwards upon myself. What a curse it is.

JESUS: Have patience Judas. Yours is the Kingdom of Heaven

Scene 6

GOD: My son, my son, he's been gone an eternity. How long it lasts! How his baby lungs concealed a lion's heart. The son of God and yet a man – O the horror of it!

I loved him as a mother loves her baby. So few were his faults also that it is true to say I loved him all the more. For his goodness, his grace, his sweetness, his wit, his wisdom, his irony and his anger. His human strengths and weaknesses. I loved him in a way, you know, you can never love yourself.

But when I sent him to be born and let him disappear, I cannot tell you where, I forgot that since each moment is an eternity I am in the strange position of enjoying his eternal presence and suffering his eternal absence.

A great many things keep happening, some of them good, some of them bad.

ACT FIVE

Scene 1

HEROD: ...but before you deliver him up to us do you think you could get him to do some miracles? I'd love to see it – to see the dead walk. Do you often see marvels in this sect of yours?

JUDAS: Oh often Great Herod, great marvels. For us the air is always full of noises. Sometimes the master, for that is what we call him, brings great troops of angels into the sky to amuse us, each of them blowing a horn. For us the days are so full of marvels that sometimes we can't tell if we awake or asleep, we are so filled with the Holy spirit that we can imagine anything we like and it may become real. We only have to ask and it shall be given to us. Such riches that you, and my great Lord Pilate, haven't seen

PILATE: Surely not greater than the riches in Rome?

JUDAS: Of course. Although it's not always what you might expect. Things keep changing you see

HEROD: They do?

JUDAS: Yes, a rich man can become a poor man – just like that. Take today for example, this morning I was a rich man

PILATE: You? But you are a poor Jew.

JUDAS: I know but there it is. I was rich, like I said, one of the richest men who ever lived, whereas this evening I am very poor

PILATE: I can see that, which is why I thought thirty pieces of silver might be useful

JUDAS: Oh, yes, thank you that's wonderful. Of course I may become very rich again.

HEROD: You might?

JUDAS: Yes, with us you see, if you become low enough you might end up very high. I'm aiming to get as low as you can possibly get.

PILATE: This is perverse, this sect. What for?

JUDAS: Because then in Heaven I might become Caesar

PILATE: Careful now young man, or you may end up in trouble also

HEROD: Yes, be careful. And how is that trick supposed to work?

JUDAS: You know when you feel really weak

HEROD: No, I always feel strong

JUDAS: Well, *if* you were to feel weak and afraid

HEROD: Afraid of what?

JUDAS: Pain, Death, Loneliness. Or just being.

HEROD: I delight in all these things

PILATE: This is a religion for weaklings?

JUDAS: Exactly, the Scum, the lowest

PILATE: Good. Go on.

JUDAS: So when we get these feelings Jesus says to us – don't worry because one day you will be as mighty as Caesar

PILATE: Does he now?

JUDAS: ...but probably not until after you are dead

HEROD: He's an imbecile is he?

JUDAS: Sort of. But so am I, and he helps me you see, because he knows that scum like me will end up on the top one day

PILATE: What? On top of what?

JUDAS: All this will be mine, the earth, your dominions, your money, it will all fall into my hands. And do you know what I'll do with it? I'll tie it all up in a bag and hang it from a tree like a dead cat

PILATE: You had better take us to him now

JUDAS: Yes but watch out as we approach him, he might fly away, or turn everyone to stone or into a flock of pigs because you have been drunk together all day haven't you like a couple of shy lovers before the act and he's bound to smell the wine on your breaths when you question him and he doesn't approve of wine, he insists on water you know for everyone, so he may not answer you, and if he does you mustn't listen too closely because he's very witty and he'll tie you up into knots, yes he will so keep a steady course and if all goes well it will soon be over just as if nothing had happened and he had never existed and we'll be able to sleep safely in our beds, because that's another thing he does, he comes in the night when you are least expecting it, and he steals your bed.

Scene 2

JESUS: O Lord take this cup from my lips. I fear them, these men. When I studied in the temple I thought the old men would take me to their hearts and love me, for their concerns were my concerns. I loved their old world religion more even than they did. When I saw a beam out of place I wanted to replace it, when I heard the old notes sung falsely, I wanted to write again the historic melodies. But they tore down your temple and put a market there. And I flung their gold in their faces so that they called *me* rebel and blasphemer. But they are the ruffians and I was the old man.

But now, near the end of my life I look back at my creations, my few words that I thought were so well chosen and I see they say nothing, and I think to myself; those old fools in their robes and with their hypocrisy are still less pompous than I, these canny villains know more than I, my secrets are obscure, my speeches are naive. I am the fool who tries to hide what he doesn't know to begin with.

GOD: Well Jesus, nobody's perfect

JESUS: Why didn't you make me better than I am?

GOD: So that you could know what they all feel like.

JESUS: Why aren't you better than you are Father?

GOD: You are too far off knowing that for me to tell you.

JESUS: Why must I go through with this futile gesture?

GOD: Just as all men have to persevere with their lives

JESUS: Will they see any meaning in what I am about to do?

GOD: For a time. Then it will fade away, quite suddenly, just as I will have faded away

JESUS: Can't I do something less…far-fetched?

GOD: No, I like the symmetry of this, its poetical.

JESUS: Its only symmetrical in that it reflects your original mistake of blaming them in the first place, for how you made them, which was your fault, not theirs.

GOD: You don't think this will work?

JESUS: Only if they thought the evil comes from themselves, or if they see me as a Saviour come in from the outside to save them from the consequences of their actions. But if this Saviour is also responsible for their actions he must be a hypocrite or at war with himself.

GOD: What have you told them?

JESUS: I have told them I am sent by my father, and my father is you, the God of Israel, the God of Moses and Abraham, the warmongering favouritising God who cares nothing for the Gentiles, who deliberately hardened the poor Pharo's heart against His people just so that He could make an example of him with plagues and frogs. No, the only reasonable thing I could tell them would be that I have been sent by way of apology, by which my father takes back upon himself, the guilt for their sins

GOD: You think so?

JESUS: But in that case it seems somewhat ungracious to accompany the apology with such stern threats of damnation if it is not accepted. And it still begs the question; if it's your fault, why not forgive them anyway, cross or no cross?

GOD: This is for them, not for me. I can forgive them if I like, and indeed I shall judge them in accordance with my secret justice which no man, not even you Jesus, can know. But man is not God and he judges himself according to his own nature. When he does wrong, does he say to himself; God has made me in such and such a way and therefore I can't help it? No, he will justify himself, praise himself for his decision, or he will feel remorse. Either way he gives himself alone the credit or the blame. Especially the intellectuals, the non-believers, they are really alone with their sin; this is what I mean by lost sheep.

JESUS: So as far as you are concerned, its not necessary?

GOD: Not for me no, but for them. It will really appeal to them, you wait and see.

JESUS: (*Somewhat pained.*) Really? Why?

GOD: It bears the imprint of their natures, they whistle it's tune to themselves in their sleep, and so do I. It is after all, my imperfection I have recreated in them, this sin and evil

JESUS: Then I shouldn't tell them God is good?

GOD: Why would I be different from all my creations? 'by your fruits shall ye be known' They name me good after that part of themselves that strives after goodness, that can *imagine* goodness. That part of their natures I share also. I too can imagine Goodness. My universe is striving after it. I am the bear following its own breath in the forest, I am the wild and the tranquil sea, and the storm and the watering rains. I am the beginning and the end, the implosion and the explosion, the crooked and the straight, the up and the down, the breadth and the height and the depth. And I am man. Insofar as these things are good, I am good

JESUS: I have said also that you are love

GOD: Perhaps it would be better to say that I am the Most of all things in the universe, including love, and if there is anyone who believes that love can perhaps be the overcoming power, then it's definitely Me who is that love

JESUS: Em...

GOD: For all my creations are an extension of myself, and indeed if I could not love these things, who could?

JESUS: Good, because if the whole of you were to be found in your creation and you were not more than it, then, I hope you realise, you wouldn't exist?

GOD: Except that in that case it would be only in Me that this phenomenon of non-existence could be found, so by your reasoning I would exist again

JESUS: Thereby ceasing to exist once more

GOD: You have the sophistry of a man

JESUS: So do you

GOD: Naturally

Pause.

JESUS: If I do this thing then, and then in men's minds you fade away, what then?

GOD: Then by a paradox, which you discovered earlier, you will live on, The Great Ironic Hero, The Redeemer King, who saved them from a God whose very unjustness, so like to their own, disqualifies him from existence. I will have become like unto man, and you my son, the son of man, will have become like unto a God. Their fondness for you will be matched only by their hatred for each other, especially those among them who most remind them of Me, my chosen people.

JESUS: And what happens when the paradox can no longer hold?

GOD: Then you will become like again unto man, and man will become like unto Me, a god. But a god like the old God, the God of the desert and the stolen herds, the God of plagues and cruel justice, for the one man to visit upon the other, The god who says; you are my people, holy in my sight; a God who is neither good nor bad but defined only by his being; This will be Man, living in the ruins of his philosophy; dancing on a pin-prick, crying out 'O Scope of my intellect', measuring out his freedom with the lengths of his chains. The dumb fucker

JESUS: How long will this take?

GOD: Two thousand years... Starting from now, – here they come.

JESUS: O God!

Enter JUDAS, accompanied a few paces behind by the SPY and the MOCKER dressed as Pontius Pilate and King Herod.

JUDAS: Who were you talking to, Jesus?

JESUS: I was talking to your God

JUDAS: *My* God?

JESUS: I feel sure of it.

JUDAS: And what about your God?

JESUS: He doesn't exist

JUDAS: Thank you Jesus, thank you Lord (*Kisses him with affection and gratitude.*)

JESUS is arrested in silence and taken away.

JUDAS calmly and quietly attempts to pray to his God.

The End.